Animals of the World

Woolly Monkey

By Edana Eckart

Children's Press®
A Division of Scholastic Inc.
New York / Toronto / London / Auckland / Sydney
Mexico City / New Delhi / Hong Kong
Danbury, Connecticut

Photo Credits: Cover, p. 7 © Kevin Schafer/Corbis; p. 5 © J. & P. Wegner/Animals Animals; p. 9 © Robert Maier/Animals Animals; p. 11 © Erwin and Peggy Bauer/Animals Animals; p. 13 © M. Watson/ardea.com; p. 15 © Zig Leszczynski/Animals Animals; p. 17 © Miriam Agron/Animals Animals; p. 19 © John Chellman/Animals Animals; p. 21 © Charles Cangialosi/Index Stock Imagery, Inc.
Contributing Editor: Shira Laskin
Book Design: Christopher Logan

Library of Congress Cataloging-in-Publication Data

Eckart, Edana.
    Woolly monkey / by Edana Eckart.
    p. cm. — (Animals of the world)
    Includes index.
    ISBN 0-516-25055-8 (lib. bdg.) — ISBN 0-516-25168-6 (pbk.)
    1. Woolly monkeys — Juvenile literature. I. Title.

    QL737.P925E34 2005
    599.8'58—dc22

                                                    2004002338

Contents

Woolly monkeys live in **rain forests** in **South America**.

They spend most of their time in trees.

5

Woolly monkeys have **thick, woolly** fur.

Woolly monkeys have long, strong tails.

They use their tails to hang from trees.

9

Woolly monkeys call out to each other.

They yell when there is **danger**.

11

Woolly monkeys walk on two legs.

13

Woolly monkeys live in groups.

Together, they look for food.

15

Woolly monkeys like to eat fruit.

17

Young woolly monkeys like to play in trees.

19

Many of the rain forests that woolly monkeys live in are being cut down.

People work to save the rain forests and take care of woolly monkeys.

New Words

danger (**dayn**-juhr) when something might happen that could hurt you

rain forests (**rayn for**-uhsts) forests in warm places with a lot of rain

South America (**south** uh-**mer**-uh-kuh) a continent below North America

thick (**thik**) filling up a lot of space from side to side or top to bottom

woolly (**wul**-ee) having soft, thick hair

woolly monkeys (**wul**-ee **muhn**-keez) large monkeys with thick fur that live in South America

To Find Out More

Books

Monkeys
by JoAnn Early Macken
Gareth Stevens Publishing

They Call Me Woolly: What Animal Names Can Tell Us
by Keith Du Quette
Penguin Group Inc.

Web Site

America Zoo: Woolly Monkey
http://www.americazoo.com/goto/index/mammals/99.htm
Learn about the woolly monkey and other animals on this
informative Web site.

Index

About the Author
Edana Eckart is a freelance writer. She has written many books about animals.

Reading Consultants
Kris Flynn, Coordinator, Small School District Literacy, The San Diego County Office of Education

Shelly Forys, Certified Reading Recovery Specialist, W.J. Zahnow Elementary School, Waterloo, IL

Paulette Mansell, Certified Reading Recovery Specialist, and Early Literacy Consultant, TX